Table of Contents

W9-AWY-716

Wings 'N' Things

Thai Chicken Wings

1 tablespoon peanut oil

5 pounds chicken wings, tips removed and split at the joint

½ cup unsweetened canned coconut milk

1 tablespoon sugar

1 tablespoon Thai green curry paste

1 tablespoon fish sauce

¾ cup prepared spicy peanut sauce

1. Heat oil in large nonstick skillet over medium-high heat. Working in batches, brown wings on all sides. Transfer to **CROCK-POT®** slow cooker.

2. Stir in coconut milk, sugar, curry paste and fish sauce. Cover; cook on LOW 6 to 7 hours or on HIGH 3 to 3½ hours or until tender. Drain off cooking liquid. Carefully stir in peanut sauce before serving.

Makes 8 servings

Mini Swiss Steak Sandwiches

2 tablespoons all-purpose flour
¼ teaspoon salt
¼ teaspoon black pepper
1¾ pounds boneless beef chuck steak, about 1 inch thick
2 tablespoons vegetable oil
1 onion, sliced
1 green bell pepper, cut into strips
1 clove garlic, sliced
1 cup stewed tomatoes
¾ cup condensed beef consommé, undiluted
2 teaspoons Worcestershire sauce
1 bay leaf
2 tablespoons cornstarch
2 packages (12 ounces each) sweet Hawaiian dinner rolls

1. Coat **CROCK-POT®** slow cooker with nonstick cooking spray. Combine flour, salt and black pepper in large resealable food storage bag. Add steak; shake to coat.

2. Heat oil in large skillet over high heat. Brown steak on both sides. Transfer to **CROCK-POT®** slow cooker.

3. Add onion and bell pepper to same skillet; cook and stir over medium-high heat 3 minutes or until softened. Add garlic; cook and stir 30 seconds. Pour mixture over steak.

4. Add tomatoes, consommé, Worcestershire sauce and bay leaf. Cover; cook on HIGH 3½ hours or until steak is tender. Transfer steak to cutting board. Remove and discard bay leaf.

5. Whisk 2 tablespoons cooking liquid into cornstarch in small bowl until smooth. Stir into cooking liquid in **CROCK-POT®** slow cooker; cover and cook on HIGH 10 minutes or until thickened.

6. Thinly slice steak against the grain. Return steak to **CROCK-POT®** slow cooker; mix well. Serve steak mixture on rolls.

Tip
Browning meat and poultry before cooking them in the **CROCK-POT®** slow cooker isn't necessary but helps to enhance the flavor and appearance of the finished dish.

Makes 16 to 18 servings

Thai Coconut Chicken Meatballs

1 **pound ground chicken**
2 **green onions, chopped**
1 **clove garlic, minced**
2 **teaspoons dark sesame oil**
2 **teaspoons mirin**
1 **teaspoon fish sauce**
1 **tablespoon canola oil**
½ **cup unsweetened canned coconut milk**
¼ **cup chicken broth**
2 **teaspoons packed brown sugar**
1 **teaspoon Thai red curry paste**
2 **teaspoons lime juice**
2 **tablespoons water**
1 **tablespoon cornstarch**

1. Combine chicken, green onions, garlic, sesame oil, mirin and fish sauce in large bowl. Shape into 1½-inch meatballs.

2. Heat canola oil in large skillet over medium-high heat. Working in batches, brown meatballs on all sides. Transfer to **CROCK-POT®** slow cooker. Add coconut milk, broth, brown sugar and curry paste. Cover; cook on HIGH 3½ to 4 hours. Stir in lime juice.

3. Stir water into cornstarch in small bowl until smooth. Stir into sauce in **CROCK-POT®** slow cooker. Cook, uncovered, on HIGH 10 to 15 minutes or until sauce is slightly thickened.

Tip
Meatballs that are of equal size will cook at the same rate and be done at the same time. To ensure your meatballs are the same size, pat seasoned ground meat into an even rectangle and then slice into even rows and columns. Roll each portion into smooth ball.

Makes 4 to 5 servings

Shrimp Fondue Dip

1 pound medium raw shrimp, peeled

½ cup water

½ teaspoon salt, divided

2 tablespoons butter, softened

4 teaspoons Dijon mustard

6 slices thick-sliced white bread, crusts removed*

1 cup milk

2 eggs, beaten

¼ teaspoon black pepper

2 cups (8 ounces) shredded Gruyére or Swiss cheese

Crusty French bread, sliced

Thick-sliced bread is often sold as "Texas Toast" in supermarket bread aisles.

1. Coat **CROCK-POT®** slow cooker with nonstick cooking spray. Place shrimp, water and ¼ teaspoon salt in small saucepan. Cover; cook over medium heat 3 minutes or until shrimp are pink and opaque. Drain shrimp, reserving ½ cup broth.

2. Combine butter and mustard in small bowl. Spread mixture onto bread slices. Cut bread into 1-inch cubes.

3. Beat milk, eggs, reserved ½ cup broth, remaining ¼ teaspoon salt and pepper in small bowl.

4. Spread one third of bread cubes in bottom of **CROCK-POT®** slow cooker. Top with one third of shrimp. Sprinkle with one third of cheese. Repeat layers twice. Pour egg mixture over top. Press down on bread mixture to absorb liquid. Line lid with two paper towels. Cover; cook on LOW 2 hours or until mixture is heated through and thickened. Serve with French bread.

Tip

For easy entertaining, use a **CROCK-POT®** slow cooker on the LOW or WARM setting to keep dips and fondues warm.

Makes 5 cups

Cereal Snack Mix

6 tablespoons unsalted butter, melted
2 tablespoons curry powder
2 tablespoons reduced-sodium soy sauce
1 tablespoon sugar
1 tablespoon paprika
2 teaspoons ground cumin
½ teaspoon salt
5 cups rice squares cereal
5 cups corn squares cereal
1 cup tiny pretzels
⅓ cup lightly salted peanuts

1. Pour butter into **CROCK-POT®** slow cooker. Stir in curry powder, soy sauce, sugar, paprika, cumin and salt. Add cereal, pretzels and peanuts; toss to coat. Cook, uncovered, on HIGH 45 minutes, stirring often to avoid scorching.

2. Turn **CROCK-POT®** slow cooker to LOW. Cook, uncovered, 3 to 4 hours, stirring often. Let cool completely.

Makes 20 servings

Tomato Topping for Bruschetta

6 medium tomatoes, peeled, seeded and diced

2 stalks celery, chopped

2 shallots, chopped

4 pepperoncini peppers, chopped*

2 teaspoons tomato paste

1 teaspoon salt

½ teaspoon black pepper

2 tablespoons olive oil

8 slices country bread or other large round bread

2 cloves garlic

Pepperoncini are pickled peppers sold in jars with brine. They're available in the supermarket condiment aisle.

1. Drain off any tomato juices. Combine tomatoes, celery, shallots, pepperoncini peppers, tomato paste, salt, black pepper and oil in **CROCK-POT**® slow cooker. Cover; cook on LOW 45 minutes to 1 hour.

2. Toast bread. Immediately rub with garlic. Spread tomato topping on bread. Serve immediately.

Makes 8 servings

Variation
To serve as a main dish, omit bread and garlic, and toss tomato topping with cooked penne pasta. You may also spoon the topping over roasted chicken breasts as a flavorful sauce.

Brats in Beer

1½ pounds bratwurst (about 5 or 6 links)
1 bottle (12 ounces) amber ale or lager
1 onion, thinly sliced
2 tablespoons packed light brown sugar
2 tablespoons red wine or cider vinegar
  Spicy brown mustard
  Cocktail rye bread

1. Combine bratwurst, ale, onion, brown sugar and vinegar in **CROCK-POT®** slow cooker. Cover; cook on LOW 4 to 5 hours.

2. Remove bratwurst from cooking liquid. Cut into ½-inch-thick slices.

3. To make mini open-faced sandwiches, spread mustard on cocktail rye bread. Top with bratwurst slices and onion. (Whole bratwursts also can be served on toasted split French or Italian rolls.)

Makes 30 to 36 appetizers

Tip
Choose a light-colored beer when cooking brats. Hearty ales can leave the meat tasting slightly bitter.

Ultimate Beef Stew

Beef Stew

½ cup all-purpose flour
1 teaspoon salt
1 teaspoon black pepper
4 pounds boneless beef chuck roast, cut into 1-inch cubes
Olive oil
2 cups dry red or white wine
1 cup beef broth
2 onions, sliced
1 cup sliced mushrooms
1 cup fresh Italian parsley, minced
6 teaspoons minced garlic
4 bay leaves

1. Combine flour, salt and pepper in large bowl. Add beef; toss to coat. Heat oil in large skillet over medium heat. Working in batches, brown beef on all sides. Transfer to **CROCK-POT®** slow cooker.

2. Add remaining ingredients; mix well. Cover; cook on LOW 4 to 6 hours or on HIGH 2 to 3 hours. Remove and discard bay leaves before serving.

Makes 6 to 8 servings

Rustic Beef and Ale Ragoût

1 tablespoon extra virgin olive oil

1½ pounds boneless beef chuck roast, cut into 1½-inch cubes

1 yellow onion, cut into ½-inch wedges

1 cup sliced carrots (about ¼-inch slices)

1 green bell pepper, sliced

12 ounces beer, preferably ale

1 can (6 ounces) tomato paste

1 package (about 1 ounce) Italian salad dressing mix

2 teaspoons beef bouillon granules

2 teaspoons Worcestershire sauce

1 teaspoon sugar

Salt and black pepper

Hot mashed potatoes (optional)

1. Coat **CROCK-POT®** slow cooker with nonstick cooking spray.

2. Heat oil in large skillet over medium-high heat. Working in batches, brown beef on all sides. Transfer to **CROCK-POT®** slow cooker. Add onion, carrots and bell pepper.

3. Return skillet to medium-high heat. Whisk in beer, tomato paste, salad dressing mix, bouillon, Worcestershire sauce and sugar. Cook until smooth, whisking to scrape up any browned bits. Pour over beef and vegetables; mix well. Cover; cook on HIGH 4 hours or until beef is tender. Season with salt and black pepper. Serve over mashed potatoes, if desired.

Makes 6 servings

French Beef Bourguignon

2 tablespoons vegetable oil

2 pounds boneless beef chuck roast, cut into 1-inch cubes

4 carrots, quartered lengthwise and cut into 4-inch pieces

1 can (about 14 ounces) diced tomatoes

1 yellow onion, diced

2 stalks celery, sliced

1 cup chopped mushrooms

1 cup dry red wine

1 tablespoon chopped fresh thyme

1 teaspoon salt

1 teaspoon minced fresh basil

1 teaspoon ground mustard

¼ teaspoon black pepper

¼ cup water

2 tablespoons all-purpose flour

1 package (16 ounces) wide egg noodles, cooked according to package directions (optional)

1. Heat oil in large skillet over medium-high heat. Working in batches, brown beef on all sides. Transfer to **CROCK-POT®** slow cooker.

2. Add carrots, tomatoes, onion, celery, mushrooms, wine, thyme, salt, basil, ground mustard and pepper; mix well. Cover; cook on LOW 8 to 10 hours or on HIGH 4 to 5 hours, or until beef is tender.

3. Thirty minutes before serving, whisk water into flour in small bowl until smooth. Stir into cooking liquid in **CROCK-POT®** slow cooker. Cook, uncovered, on HIGH 5 minutes or until thickened. Serve over noodles, if desired.

Makes 8 servings

Greek Braised Beef Stew

¼ cup all-purpose flour

2 teaspoons Greek seasoning

¼ teaspoon salt

¼ teaspoon black pepper

2 pounds beef stew meat or boneless beef chuck roast, cut into 1-inch cubes

2 tablespoons olive oil

2 cups beef broth

2 onions, each cut into 8 wedges

1 container (10 ounces) grape or cherry tomatoes

1 jar (8 ounces) pitted kalamata olives, drained

8 sprigs fresh oregano, divided

1 lemon, divided

1. Combine flour, seasoning, salt and pepper in large resealable food storage bag. Add beef; shake to coat. Heat oil in large skillet over medium-high heat. Working in batches, brown beef on all sides. Transfer to **CROCK-POT®** slow cooker.

2. Add broth, onions, tomatoes, olives, 4 sprigs oregano and juice of ½ lemon. Cover; cook on HIGH 6 to 7 hours or until beef is tender. Cut remaining ½ lemon into wedges and serve with stew. Garnish with remaining oregano.

Tip
Spinning or tapping the cover until the condensation falls off will allow you to see inside the **CROCK-POT®** slow cooker without removing the lid, which lengthens the cooking time.

Makes 6 servings

Asian Beef Stew

2 onions, cut into ¼-inch slices

1½ pounds boneless beef round steak, sliced thin across the grain

2 stalks celery, sliced

2 carrots, sliced

1 cup sliced mushrooms

1 cup orange juice

1 cup beef broth

⅓ cup hoisin sauce

2 tablespoons cornstarch

1 to 2 teaspoons Chinese five-spice powder or curry powder

1 cup frozen peas

Hot cooked rice

Chopped fresh cilantro (optional)

1. Layer onions, beef, celery, carrots and mushrooms in **CROCK-POT®** slow cooker.

2. Combine orange juice, broth, hoisin sauce, cornstarch and five-spice powder in small bowl. Pour into **CROCK-POT®** slow cooker. Cover; cook on HIGH 5 hours or until beef is tender.

3. Stir in peas. Cover; cook on HIGH 20 minutes or until peas are tender. Serve over rice. Garnish with cilantro.

Makes 6 servings

Easy Beef Burgundy

1½ pounds boneless beef round steak or beef stew meat, cut into 1-inch cubes

1 can (10¾ ounces) condensed cream of mushroom soup, undiluted

1 cup dry red wine

1 onion, chopped

1 can (4 ounces) sliced mushrooms, drained

1 package (about 1 ounce) dry onion soup mix

1 tablespoon minced garlic

Combine all ingredients in **CROCK-POT**® slow cooker. Cover; cook on LOW 6 to 8 hours or until beef is tender.

Makes 4 to 6 servings

Autumn Apricot Beef Ragoût

1 pound boneless beef round steak, cut into bite-size pieces

1 cup medium chunky salsa

⅔ cup apricot nectar

1 teaspoon pumpkin pie spice

¼ teaspoon salt

½ cup chopped dried apricots

½ cup sliced green onions

3 tablespoons water

2 tablespoons all-purpose flour

3 cups hot cooked rice

¼ cup chopped fresh cilantro

1. Place beef, salsa, nectar, pumpkin pie spice and salt in **CROCK-POT**® slow cooker. Cover; cook on LOW 8 to 10 hours.

2. Turn **CROCK-POT**® slow cooker to HIGH. Add apricots and green onions. Cover; cook 10 minutes.

3. Stir water into flour in small bowl until smooth. Add to **CROCK-POT**® slow cooker; mix well. Cover; cook on HIGH 15 minutes or until thickened.

4. Serve over rice. Garnish with cilantro.

Makes 3 to 4 servings

Sweet and Sour Brisket Stew

1 jar (12 ounces) chili sauce
¼ cup beef broth
1½ tablespoons packed dark brown sugar
1½ tablespoons fresh lemon juice
1 tablespoon Dijon mustard
¼ teaspoon paprika
½ teaspoon salt
¼ teaspoon black pepper
1 beef brisket, trimmed and cut into 1-inch pieces*
2 carrots, cut into ½-inch slices
1 onion, chopped
1 clove garlic, minced
1 tablespoon all-purpose flour (optional)

*Beef brisket has a heavy layer of fat, which some supermarkets trim off. If the meat is trimmed, buy 2½ pounds; if not, purchase 4 pounds, then trim and discard excess fat.

1. Combine chili sauce, broth, brown sugar, lemon juice, mustard, paprika, salt and pepper in **CROCK-POT®** slow cooker.

2. Add beef, carrots, onion and garlic; mix well. Cover; cook on LOW 8 hours.

3. For thicker gravy, turn **CROCK-POT®** slow cooker to HIGH. Stir 3 tablespoons cooking liquid into flour in small bowl until smooth. Stir into **CROCK-POT®** slow cooker. Cover; cook 10 minutes or until thickened.

Makes 6 to 8 servings

Top This!

Chinese Pork Tenderloin

2 pork tenderloins
(about 2 pounds total)

1 green bell pepper, cut
into ½-inch pieces

1 red bell pepper, cut into
½-inch pieces

1 onion, thinly sliced

2 carrots, thinly sliced

1 jar (15 ounces) sweet
and sour sauce

1 tablespoon soy sauce

½ teaspoon hot pepper
sauce

Hot cooked rice

Fresh cilantro (optional)

1. Cut pork into 1-inch cubes
and place in **CROCK-POT®**
slow cooker.

2. Add bell peppers, onion,
carrots, sweet and sour sauce,
soy sauce and hot pepper
sauce; mix well. Cover; cook
on LOW 6 to 7 hours or on
HIGH 4 to 5 hours. Stir just
before serving. Serve over rice.
Garnish with cilantro.

Makes 8 servings

Lamb Shank and Mushroom Stew

2 tablespoons olive oil, divided
2 large lamb shanks (about 2 pounds total)
2 tablespoons all-purpose flour
2 cups sliced mushrooms*
1 red onion, thinly sliced
1 clove garlic, minced
1¼ cups chicken broth
½ cup sliced pitted green olives
¼ teaspoon salt
⅛ teaspoon black pepper
⅛ teaspoon dried thyme
2 tablespoons capers, drained
Hot cooked noodles

*Shiitake mushroom caps are preferred for this dish, but you may use other mushroom varieties.

1. Heat 1 tablespoon oil in large skillet over medium-high heat. Dust lamb shanks with flour, reserving leftover flour. Brown lamb on all sides. Transfer to **CROCK-POT®** slow cooker.

2. Heat remaining 1 tablespoon oil in same skillet over medium-high heat. Add mushrooms, onion and garlic; cook and stir 3 minutes or until tender. Transfer to **CROCK-POT®** slow cooker.

3. Sprinkle reserved flour into skillet. Add broth, stirring to scrape up any browned bits. Cook and stir 2 minutes or until slightly thickened. Pour into **CROCK-POT®** slow cooker.

4. Stir in olives, salt, pepper and thyme. Cover; cook on LOW 7 to 8 hours or on HIGH 4 to 5 hours.

5. Transfer lamb to cutting board. Gently pull meat from bones with fork. Discard bones. Let cooking liquid stand 5 minutes. Skim off and discard excess fat. Return lamb to **CROCK-POT®** slow cooker. Stir in capers. Serve lamb and sauce over noodles.

Makes 4 servings

Chicken Gumbo over Rice

4 tablespoons olive oil, divided

½ pound Italian sausage, cut into ¼-inch slices

¼ cup all-purpose flour

1 pound boneless skinless chicken breasts, cut into ½-inch slices

1 cup chopped onion

1 cup chopped celery

1 cup diced green bell pepper

2 tablespoons minced jalapeño peppers*

1 teaspoon paprika

1½ cups fresh or frozen okra, cut into ¼-inch slices

1 cup chicken broth

½ cup dry white wine

Hot cooked rice

*Jalapeño peppers can sting and irritate the skin, so wear rubber gloves when handling peppers and do not touch your eyes.

1. Heat 2 tablespoons oil in large skillet over medium heat. Brown sausage, stirring to break up meat. Drain fat; transfer to paper towel-lined plate.

2. Heat remaining 2 tablespoons oil in same skillet. Add flour; whisk constantly until flour is dark brown but not burnt. Add chicken, onion, celery, bell pepper, jalapeño peppers and paprika; cook and stir 8 minutes or until softened. Transfer to **CROCK-POT®** slow cooker.

3. Add sausage, okra, broth and wine. Cover; cook on LOW 7 to 8 hours or on HIGH 4 to 6 hours. Serve over rice.

Makes 6 servings

Turkey Piccata

2½ tablespoons all-purpose flour
¼ teaspoon salt
¼ teaspoon black pepper
1 pound turkey breast meat, cut into strips*
1 tablespoon butter
1 tablespoon olive oil
½ cup chicken broth
2 teaspoons lemon juice
Grated peel of 1 lemon
Hot cooked rice
2 tablespoons finely chopped fresh parsley
*You may substitute turkey tenderloins; cut as directed.

1. Combine flour, salt and pepper in large resealable food storage bag. Add turkey; shake to coat. Heat butter and oil in large skillet over medium-high heat. Add turkey strips in single layer; brown on all sides. Transfer to **CROCK-POT®** slow cooker, arranging on bottom in single layer.

2. Pour broth into skillet, stirring to scrape up any browned bits. Pour into **CROCK-POT®** slow cooker. Add lemon juice and peel. Cover; cook on LOW 1 hour. Serve over rice. Sprinkle with parsley.

Makes 4 servings

Tip
This recipe is also great with chicken. Start with boneless skinless chicken breasts, then follow the recipe as directed.

Middle Eastern-Spiced Beef, Tomatoes and Beans

2 tablespoons extra virgin olive oil, divided

1½ pounds boneless beef chuck roast, cut into 1-inch cubes, divided

1 can (about 14 ounces) diced tomatoes with peppers and onions

6 ounces green beans, trimmed and broken into 1-inch pieces

1 cup chopped onion

1½ teaspoons sugar

½ teaspoon ground cinnamon

¼ teaspoon ground allspice

¼ teaspoon garlic powder

½ teaspoon salt

¼ teaspoon black pepper

Hot cooked couscous or rice

1. Heat 2 teaspoons oil in large skillet over medium-high heat. Working in batches, brown beef on all sides. Add additional 2 teaspoons oil as needed. Transfer to **CROCK-POT®** slow cooker.

2. Stir in tomatoes, green beans, onion, sugar, cinnamon, allspice and garlic powder. Cover; cook on LOW 8 hours or on HIGH 4 hours.

3. Stir in salt, pepper and remaining 2 teaspoons oil. Let stand, uncovered, 15 minutes to allow flavors to absorb and thicken slightly. Serve over couscous or rice.

Makes about 4 servings

Braised Italian Chicken with Tomatoes and Olives

2 pounds boneless skinless chicken thighs

1 teaspoon kosher salt

½ teaspoon black pepper

½ cup all-purpose flour
Olive oil

1 can (about 14 ounces) diced tomatoes, drained

⅓ cup quartered pitted kalamata olives

⅓ cup dry red wine

1 clove garlic, minced

1 teaspoon chopped fresh rosemary leaves

½ teaspoon red pepper flakes
Hot cooked linguine or spaghetti
Grated Parmesan cheese (optional)

1. Season chicken with salt and black pepper. Spread flour on plate. Dredge chicken in flour, coating both sides.

2. Heat oil in large skillet over medium heat. Working in batches, brown chicken on both sides. Transfer to **CROCK-POT®** slow cooker.

3. Add tomatoes, olives, wine and garlic. Cover; cook on LOW 4 to 5 hours.

4. Stir in rosemary and red pepper flakes. Cover; cook on LOW 1 hour. Serve over linguine. Garnish with cheese.

Makes 4 servings

Creamy Chicken and Mushrooms

1 teaspoon salt
½ teaspoon black pepper
¼ teaspoon paprika
3 boneless skinless chicken breasts, cut into 1-inch cubes
1½ cups sliced mushrooms
½ cup sliced green onions
1¾ teaspoons chicken bouillon granules
1 cup dry white wine
½ cup water
1 can (5 ounces) evaporated milk
5 teaspoons cornstarch
Hot cooked rice

1. Combine salt, pepper and paprika in small bowl; sprinkle over chicken.

2. Layer chicken, mushrooms, green onions and bouillon in **CROCK-POT®** slow cooker. Pour wine and water over top. Cover; cook on LOW 5 to 6 hours or on HIGH 3 hours. Transfer chicken and vegetables to platter; cover with foil to keep warm.

3. Whisk evaporated milk into cornstarch in small saucepan until smooth. Add 2 cups cooking liquid from **CROCK-POT®** slow cooker; bring to a boil over medium-high heat. Boil 1 minute or until thickened, whisking constantly. Serve chicken and sauce over rice.

Makes 3 to 4 servings

Meatballs and Spaghetti Sauce

Meatballs

- **2 pounds ground beef**
- **1 cup plain dry bread crumbs**
- **1 onion, chopped**
- **2 eggs, beaten**
- **¼ cup minced fresh Italian parsley**
- **2 teaspoons minced garlic**
- **½ teaspoon ground mustard**
- **½ teaspoon black pepper**
  Olive oil

Spaghetti Sauce

- **1 can (28 ounces) whole tomatoes**
- **½ cup chopped fresh basil**
- **2 tablespoons olive oil**
- **2 cloves garlic, finely minced**
- **1 teaspoon sugar**
  Salt and black pepper

  Hot cooked spaghetti

1. Combine all meatball ingredients except oil in large bowl. Shape into walnut-sized meatballs. Heat oil in large skillet over medium heat. Working in batches, brown meatballs on all sides. Transfer to **CROCK-POT**® slow cooker.

2. Combine all sauce ingredients in medium bowl. Pour over meatballs, stirring to coat. Cover; cook on LOW 3 to 5 hours or on HIGH 2 to 4 hours. Serve over spaghetti.

Makes 6 to 8 servings

Old World Chicken and Vegetables

1 tablespoon dried oregano

1 teaspoon salt, divided

1 teaspoon paprika

½ teaspoon garlic powder

¼ teaspoon black pepper

2 green bell peppers, cut into thin strips

1 yellow onion, thinly sliced

1 whole chicken (about 3 pounds), cut up

⅓ cup ketchup

Hot cooked egg noodles

1. Combine oregano, ½ teaspoon salt, paprika, garlic powder and black pepper in small bowl.

2. Place bell peppers and onion in **CROCK-POT®** slow cooker. Add chicken thighs and legs; sprinkle with half of oregano mixture. Add chicken breasts; sprinkle with remaining oregano mixture. Cover; cook on LOW 8 hours or on HIGH 4 hours. Stir in ketchup and remaining ½ teaspoon salt.

3. Serve chicken and vegetables over noodles.

Makes 4 servings

Mango Ginger Pork Roast

1 pork shoulder roast
(about 4 pounds)
½ to 1 teaspoon ground
ginger
Salt and black pepper
2 cups mango salsa
¼ cup apricot preserves
2 tablespoons honey
Hot cooked rice

1. Season pork with ginger, salt and pepper. Transfer to **CROCK-POT®** slow cooker.

2. Combine salsa, preserves and honey in small bowl; pour over pork. Cover; cook on LOW 6 to 8 hours. Turn **CROCK-POT®** slow cooker to HIGH. Cover; cook 3 to 4 hours or until tender. Serve over rice.

Makes 4 to 6 servings

Twice as Nice

Simmering Hot and Sour Soup

2 cans (about 14 ounces each) chicken broth
1 cup chopped cooked chicken or pork
4 ounces shiitake mushroom caps, thinly sliced
½ cup thinly sliced bamboo shoots
3 tablespoons rice wine vinegar
2 tablespoons soy sauce
1½ teaspoons chili paste *or* 1 teaspoon hot chili oil
4 ounces firm tofu, drained and cut into ½-inch pieces
2 teaspoons dark sesame oil
2 tablespoons water
2 tablespoons cornstarch
Chopped fresh cilantro or sliced green onions

1. Combine broth, chicken, mushrooms, bamboo shoots, vinegar, soy sauce and chili paste in **CROCK-POT**® slow cooker. Cover; cook on LOW 3 to 4 hours or on HIGH 2 to 3 hours or until chicken is heated through.

2. Stir in tofu and sesame oil. Whisk water into cornstarch in small bowl until smooth; stir into soup. Cover; cook on HIGH 10 minutes or until thickened. Sprinkle with cilantro.

Makes 4 servings

Tip
Serve this with Asian Lettuce Wraps (see page 42) for an easy, complete Asian meal!

Asian Lettuce Wraps

2 teaspoons canola oil

1 pound boneless skinless chicken breasts or pork shoulder, cut into ¼-inch cubes

1 leek, white and green parts, trimmed and chopped into ¼-inch pieces

¾ cup shiitake mushrooms, stems removed and caps chopped into ¼-inch pieces

1 stalk celery, chopped into ¼-inch pieces

2 teaspoons oyster sauce

2 teaspoons soy sauce

1 teaspoon dark sesame oil

⅛ teaspoon black pepper

2 tablespoons water

1 bag (8 ounces) cole slaw or broccoli slaw mix

½ red bell pepper, cut into thin strips

⅓ pound large raw shrimp, peeled, deveined and cut into ¼-inch pieces

2 tablespoons salted dry roasted peanuts, coarsely chopped
Hoisin sauce, to taste

8 to 10 leaves crisp romaine lettuce, white rib removed and patted dry
Fresh chives (optional)

1. Heat canola oil in medium skillet over medium-high heat. Brown chicken on all sides. Transfer to **CROCK-POT®** slow cooker. Add leek, mushrooms, celery, oyster sauce, soy sauce, sesame oil, black pepper and water. Toss slaw mix and bell pepper in medium bowl; place in single layer on top of chicken.

2. Cover; cook on LOW 4 to 5 hours or on HIGH 2 to 2½ hours, or until chicken is cooked through. Stir in shrimp during last 20 minutes of cooking. When shrimp are pink and opaque, transfer mixture to large bowl. Add chopped peanuts; mix well.

3. To serve, spread about 1 teaspoon hoisin sauce on lettuce leaf. Add about 1 tablespoon meat mixture and tightly roll like a cigar; secure by tying chives around rolled leaves, if desired. Alternatively, set out bowls of filling, hoisin and meat mixture for guests to roll themselves.

Makes about 4 servings

Vegetarian Chili

1 tablespoon vegetable oil

1 cup chopped onion

1 cup chopped red bell pepper

2 tablespoons minced jalapeño peppers*

1 clove garlic, minced

1 can (28 ounces) crushed tomatoes, undrained

1 can (about 15 ounces) black beans, rinsed and drained

1 can (about 15 ounces) chickpeas, rinsed and drained

½ cup corn

¼ cup tomato paste

1 teaspoon sugar

1 teaspoon ground cumin

1 teaspoon dried basil

1 teaspoon chili powder

¼ teaspoon black pepper

Sour cream and shredded Cheddar cheese (optional)

*Jalapeño peppers can sting and irritate the skin, so wear rubber gloves when handling peppers and do not touch your eyes.

1. Heat oil in large skillet over medium-high heat. Add onion, bell pepper, jalapeño peppers and garlic; cook and stir 5 minutes or until tender. Transfer to **CROCK-POT®** slow cooker.

2. Add remaining ingredients except sour cream and cheese; mix well. Cover; cook on LOW 4 to 5 hours.

3. Garnish with sour cream and cheese.

Makes 4 servings

Chorizo Chili

1 pound ground beef

8 ounces bulk raw chorizo sausage *or* ½ (15-ounce) package raw chorizo sausage, casings removed

1 can (16 ounces) chili beans in chili sauce

2 cans (about 14 ounces each) chili-style diced tomatoes

1. Place beef and chorizo in **CROCK-POT®** slow cooker. Break up with fork to form small chunks.

2. Stir in beans and tomatoes. Cover; cook on LOW 7 hours. Skim off and discard excess fat before serving.

Makes 6 servings

Serving suggestion
Top with sour cream or shredded cheese.

Sloppy Sloppy Joes

1 **pound ground beef**
¼ **cup chopped onion**
¼ **cup chopped green bell pepper**
1 **can (8 ounces) tomato sauce**
½ **cup canned condensed tomato soup, undiluted**
¼ **cup packed brown sugar**
1 **tablespoon ketchup**
1 **tablespoon Worcestershire sauce**
½ **tablespoon ground mustard**
1 **teaspoon prepared mustard**
½ **teaspoon chili powder**
¼ **teaspoon garlic powder**
  Toasted sandwich rolls

1. Brown beef in large skillet over medium-high heat, stirring to break up meat. Drain fat.

2. Add onion and bell pepper to beef; cook and stir 5 to 10 minutes or until onion is translucent. Transfer to **CROCK-POT®** slow cooker.

3. Add remaining ingredients except rolls; mix well. Cover; cook on LOW 4 to 6 hours. Serve on rolls.

Makes 4 to 5 servings

Meatless Sloppy Joes

2 cups thinly sliced onions
2 cups chopped green bell peppers
1 can (about 15 ounces) kidney beans, drained and mashed
1 can (8 ounces) tomato sauce
2 tablespoons ketchup
1 tablespoon yellow mustard
2 cloves garlic, finely chopped
1 teaspoon chili powder
Cider vinegar (optional)
4 sandwich rolls

Combine onions, bell peppers, beans, tomato sauce, ketchup, mustard, garlic and chili powder in **CROCK-POT®** slow cooker. Cover; cook on LOW 5 to 5½ hours or until vegetables are tender. Season to taste with cider vinegar, if desired. Serve on rolls.

Makes 4 servings

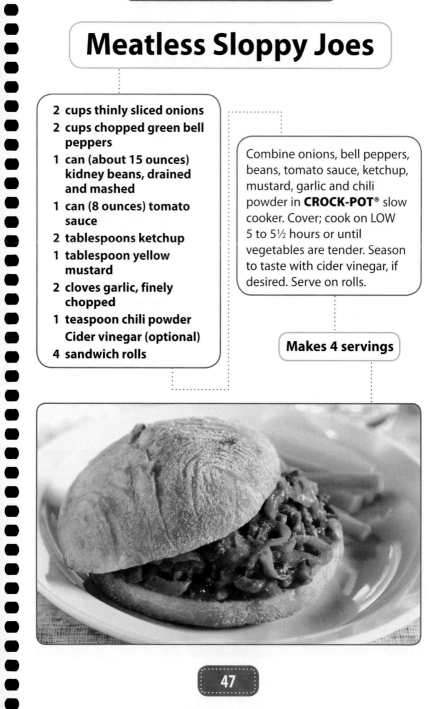

Tortilla Soup

1½ cans (about 14 ounces each) chicken broth

1½ cups chopped carrots

1½ cups frozen corn, thawed

1 cup chopped onions

¾ cup canned diced tomatoes with jalapeño peppers

¾ cup tomato sauce

2 teaspoons chili powder

½ teaspoon ground cumin

⅛ teaspoon garlic powder

1½ cups chopped cooked chicken (optional)

Combine broth, carrots, corn, onions, tomatoes, tomato sauce, chili powder, cumin and garlic powder in **CROCK-POT®** slow cooker. Cover; cook on LOW 6 to 8 hours. Stir in chicken, if desired.

Makes 4 servings

Serving Suggestion
Top with shredded Monterey Jack cheese and crushed tortilla chips.

Simple Shredded Pork Tacos

2 pounds boneless pork roast
1 cup salsa
1 can (4 ounces) chopped mild green chiles, drained
½ teaspoon garlic salt
½ teaspoon black pepper
Flour or corn tortillas
Optional toppings: salsa, sour cream, diced tomatoes, shredded cheese, shredded lettuce

1. Place pork, salsa, chiles, garlic salt and pepper in **CROCK-POT®** slow cooker, cutting pork into large pieces to fit if necessary. Cover; cook on LOW 8 hours or until pork is tender.

2. Remove pork from **CROCK-POT®** slow cooker; shred with two forks. Serve on flour tortillas with sauce. Top as desired.

Makes 6 servings

Pork Roast with Fruit Medley

½ cup water
¼ cup kosher or coarse salt
1½ teaspoons sugar
½ teaspoon dried thyme
1 bay leaf
1 boneless pork roast (about 2 pounds)
  Olive oil
1 cup green grapes
½ cup dried apricots
½ cup dried prunes
1 clove garlic, minced
½ cup dry red wine
  Juice of ¼ lemon
  Hot cooked rice or couscous

1. Combine water, salt, sugar, thyme and bay leaf in large resealable food storage bag or in plastic or glass container (do not use metal container). Add pork; Marinate in refrigerator overnight or up to 2 days, turning occasionally.

2. Drain pork; pat dry. Heat oil in large skillet over medium heat. Brown pork on all sides. Transfer to **CROCK-POT®** slow cooker, cutting in half to fit if necessary.

3. Add remaining ingredients except rice; mix well. Cover; cook on LOW 7 to 9 hours or on HIGH 3 to 5 hours. Remove and discard bay leaf. Serve over rice.

Makes about 4 servings

Rustic Garlic Mashed Potatoes

2 pounds baking potatoes, unpeeled and cut into ½-inch cubes
¼ cup water
2 tablespoons butter, cut into ⅛-inch pieces
1¼ teaspoons salt
½ teaspoon garlic powder
¼ teaspoon black pepper
1 cup milk

Place all ingredients except milk in **CROCK-POT®** slow cooker; toss to combine. Cover; cook on LOW 7 hours or on HIGH 4 hours. Add milk to potatoes. Mash potatoes with potato masher or electric mixer until smooth.

Makes 5 servings

Artichoke and Nacho Cheese Dip

2 cans (10¾ ounces each) condensed nacho cheese soup, undiluted

1 can (14 ounces) quartered artichoke hearts, drained and coarsely chopped

1 cup (4 ounces) shredded or thinly sliced pepper jack cheese

1 can (5 ounces) evaporated milk

2 tablespoons minced fresh chives, divided

½ teaspoon paprika
  Crackers or chips

1. Combine soup, artichoke hearts, cheese, milk, 1 tablespoon chives and paprika in **CROCK-POT®** slow cooker. Cover; cook on LOW 2 hours.

2. Stir well. Sprinkle with remaining 1 tablespoon chives and serve with crackers.

Makes about 1 quart

Chunky Pinto Bean Dip

2 cans (about 15 ounces each) pinto beans, rinsed and drained

1 can (about 14 ounces) diced tomatoes with mild green chiles

1 cup chopped onion

⅔ cup chunky salsa

1 tablespoon vegetable oil

1½ teaspoons minced garlic

1 teaspoon ground coriander

1 teaspoon ground cumin

1½ cups (6 ounces) shredded Mexican cheese blend or Cheddar cheese

¼ cup chopped fresh cilantro

Blue corn or other tortilla chips

Assorted raw vegetables

1. Combine beans, tomatoes, onion, salsa, oil, garlic, coriander and cumin in **CROCK-POT®** slow cooker.

2. Cover; cook on LOW 5 to 6 hours or until onion is tender.

3. Partially mash bean mixture with potato masher. Stir in cheese and cilantro. Serve at room temperature with tortilla chips and vegetables.

Makes about 5 cups

Chicken Tonight

Boneless Chicken Cacciatore

Olive oil
6 boneless skinless chicken breasts, sliced in half horizontally
4 cups tomato-basil sauce or marinara sauce
1 cup coarsely chopped yellow onion
1 cup coarsely chopped green bell pepper
1 can (6 ounces) sliced mushrooms
¼ cup dry red wine (optional)
2 teaspoons minced garlic
2 teaspoons salt
2 teaspoons dried oregano
2 teaspoons dried thyme
2 teaspoons black pepper

1. Heat oil in large skillet over medium heat. Working in batches, brown chicken on both sides. Transfer to **CROCK-POT®** slow cooker.

2. Add remaining ingredients; mix well. Cover; cook on LOW 5 to 7 hours or on HIGH 2 to 3 hours.

Makes 8 servings

Easy Cheesy Aruban-Inspired Chicken

1 can (about 14 ounces) diced tomatoes

½ cup chicken broth

¼ cup ketchup

2 teaspoons yellow mustard

1 teaspoon Worcestershire sauce

¾ teaspoon hot pepper sauce

3 cloves garlic, crushed

½ teaspoon salt

¼ teaspoon black pepper

1 onion, thinly sliced

1 green bell pepper, thinly sliced

¼ cup sliced pitted black olives

¼ cup raisins

1 tablespoon capers, drained

4 to 6 chicken thighs *or* 4 boneless skinless chicken breasts

1½ cups (6 ounces) shredded Edam or Gouda cheese

2 tablespoons chopped fresh Italian parsley

Hot cooked rice (optional)

1. Coat **CROCK-POT®** slow cooker with nonstick cooking spray. Add tomatoes, broth, ketchup, mustard, Worcestershire sauce, hot pepper sauce, garlic, salt and black pepper; mix well.

2. Add onion, bell pepper, olives, raisins and capers; mix well.

3. Add chicken. Spoon sauce mixture over chicken until well coated. Cover; cook on HIGH 3 to 4 hours or until chicken is fork-tender.

4. Turn off **CROCK-POT®** slow cooker. Uncover; sprinkle cheese and parsley over chicken. Cover; let stand 3 to 5 minutes or until cheese is melted. Serve over rice, if desired.

Makes 4 servings

Curry Chicken with Mango and Red Pepper

6 boneless skinless chicken thighs or breasts
  Salt and black pepper
  Olive oil
1 bag (8 ounces) frozen mango chunks, thawed and drained
2 red bell peppers, diced
⅓ cup raisins
1 shallot, thinly sliced
¾ cup chicken broth
1 tablespoon cider vinegar
2 cloves garlic, crushed
4 thin slices fresh ginger
1 teaspoon ground cumin
½ teaspoon curry powder
½ teaspoon whole cloves
¼ teaspoon ground red pepper (optional)
  Fresh cilantro (optional)

1. Rinse, dry and season chicken with salt and black pepper.

2. Heat oil in large skillet over medium heat. Brown chicken on both sides. Transfer to **CROCK-POT®** slow cooker.

3. Add mango, bell peppers, raisins and shallot to **CROCK-POT®** slow cooker. Combine remaining ingredients in small bowl; pour over chicken. Cover; cook on LOW 6 to 8 hours or on HIGH 3 to 4 hours.

4. To serve, spoon mangos, raisins and cooking liquid onto chicken. Garnish with cilantro.

Makes 4 to 6 servings

Chicken Parmesan with Eggplant

6 **boneless skinless chicken breasts**

2 **eggs**

2 **teaspoons salt**

2 **teaspoons black pepper**

2 **cups Italian seasoned dry bread crumbs**

½ **cup olive oil**

½ **cup (1 stick) butter**

2 **small eggplants, cut into ¾-inch-thick slices**

1½ **cups grated Parmesan cheese, divided**

2½ **cups tomato-basil sauce, divided**

1 **pound sliced or shredded mozzarella cheese**

1. Slice chicken breasts in half lengthwise. Cut each half lengthwise again to get 4 (¾-inch) slices.

2. Combine eggs, salt and pepper in medium bowl. Place bread crumbs in separate bowl or on plate. Dip chicken in egg, then coat in bread crumbs.

3. Heat oil and butter in large skillet over medium heat. Working in batches, brown chicken on all sides. Transfer to paper towel-lined plate.

4. Layer eggplant on bottom of **CROCK-POT®** slow cooker. Add ¾ cup Parmesan cheese and 1¼ cups sauce. Arrange chicken on sauce. Add remaining Parmesan cheese and sauce. Top with mozzarella cheese. Cover; cook on LOW 6 hours or on HIGH 2 to 4 hours.

Makes 6 to 8 servings

Chicken Tangier

2 tablespoons dried oregano

2 teaspoons seasoning salt

2 teaspoons puréed garlic

¼ teaspoon black pepper

8 skinless chicken thighs (about 3 pounds)

1 lemon, thinly sliced

½ cup dry white wine

2 tablespoons olive oil

1 cup pitted prunes

¼ cup currants or raisins

½ cup pitted green olives

2 tablespoons capers, drained

Couscous

Chopped fresh parsley or cilantro (optional)

1. Combine oregano, salt, garlic and pepper in small bowl. Rub onto chicken, coating all sides.

2. Coat **CROCK-POT**® slow cooker with nonstick cooking spray. Arrange chicken inside, tucking lemon slices between pieces. Pour wine over chicken and drizzle with oil. Add prunes, currants, olives and capers. Cover; cook on LOW 7 to 8 hours or on HIGH 4 to 5 hours.

3. Serve over couscous. Garnish with parsley.

Makes 8 servings

Tip
It may seem like a lot, but this recipe really does call for 2 tablespoons dried oregano in order to more accurately represent the rich flavors of Moroccan food.

Like Grandma's Chicken 'n' Dumplings

2 cups cooked chicken

1 can (10¾ ounces) condensed cream of mushroom soup, undiluted

1 can (10¾ ounces) condensed cream of chicken soup, undiluted

2 soup cans water

4 teaspoons all-purpose flour

2 teaspoons chicken bouillon granules

½ teaspoon black pepper

1 can refrigerated buttermilk biscuits (8 biscuits)

1. Mix all ingredients except biscuits in **CROCK-POT**® slow cooker.

2. Cut biscuits into quarters and gently stir into mixture. Cover; cook on LOW 4 to 6 hours.

Makes 4 to 6 servings

Citrus Mangoretto Chicken

4 boneless skinless chicken breasts (about 1 pound)
1 large ripe mango, diced
3 tablespoons lime juice
1 tablespoon grated lime peel
¼ cup Amaretto liqueur
1 tablespoon chopped fresh rosemary leaves *or* 1 teaspoon crushed dried rosemary
1 cup chicken broth
1 tablespoon water
2 teaspoons cornstarch

1. Place two chicken breasts side by side on bottom of **CROCK-POT®** slow cooker.

2. Combine mango, lime juice, lime peel, Amaretto and rosemary in medium bowl. Spread half of mango mixture over chicken in **CROCK-POT®** slow cooker. Lay remaining two chicken breasts on top crosswise; spread with remaining mango mixture. Carefully pour broth around edges of chicken. Cover; cook on LOW 3 to 4 hours.

3. Whisk water into cornstarch. in small bowl until smooth. Stir into cooking liquid. Cook on LOW 15 minutes or until thickened. Serve mango and sauce over chicken.

Makes 4 servings

Variation
Chill chicken and sauce. Serve over salad greens.

Chicken and Ham with Biscuits

2 cans (10¾ ounces each) condensed cream of mushroom soup, undiluted

2 cups diced ham

2 cups diced boneless chicken

1 package (12 ounces) frozen peas and onions

1 package (8 ounces) frozen corn

½ cup chopped celery

¼ teaspoon dried marjoram

¼ teaspoon dried thyme

2 teaspoons water

2 tablespoons cornstarch

1 to 2 cans refrigerated buttermilk biscuits (8 biscuits)

¼ cup (½ stick) butter, melted

1. Combine soup, ham, chicken, frozen vegetables, celery, marjoram and thyme in **CROCK-POT®** slow cooker. Cover; cook on LOW 4 to 5 hours or on HIGH 1 to 3 hours.

2. Whisk water into cornstarch in small bowl until smooth. Stir into **CROCK-POT®** slow cooker. Cover; cook on LOW 10 to 15 minutes or until thickened.

3. Meanwhile, place biscuits on baking sheet and brush with butter. Bake according to package directions until biscuits are golden brown.

4. To serve, split biscuits in half. Ladle stew onto biscuit bottoms and top with other half.

Makes 8 to 10 servings

Chicken Vesuvio

3 tablespoons all-purpose flour

1½ teaspoons dried oregano

1 teaspoon salt

½ teaspoon black pepper

1 whole chicken, cut up *or* 3 pounds bone-in chicken pieces

2 tablespoons olive oil

4 small baking potatoes, scrubbed, cut into 8 wedges each

2 onions, cut into thin wedges

4 cloves garlic, minced

¼ cup chicken broth

¼ cup dry white wine

¼ cup chopped fresh parsley

Lemon wedges (optional)

1. Combine flour, oregano, salt and pepper in large resealable food storage bag. Add chicken to bag, several pieces at a time; shake to coat. Heat oil in large skillet over medium heat. Working in batches, brown chicken on all sides.

2. Place potatoes, onions and garlic in **CROCK-POT**® slow cooker. Pour in broth and wine. Top with chicken pieces; pour pan juices from skillet over chicken. Cover; cook on LOW 6 to 7 hours or on HIGH 3 to 3½ hours, or until chicken and potatoes are tender.

3. Transfer chicken and vegetables to plates; top with cooking liquid from **CROCK-POT**® slow cooker. Sprinkle with parsley. Serve with lemon wedges, if desired.

Makes 4 to 6 servings

Chicken Saltimbocca-Style

- 6 **boneless skinless chicken breasts**
- 12 **slices prosciutto**
- 12 **slices provolone cheese**
- ½ **cup all-purpose flour**
- ½ **cup grated Parmesan cheese**
- 2 **teaspoons salt**
- 2 **teaspoons black pepper**
  Olive oil
- 2 **cans (10¾ ounces each) condensed cream of mushroom soup, undiluted**
- ¾ **cup white wine (optional)**
- 1 **teaspoon ground sage**

1. Slice each chicken breast into two thin pieces. Place between two pieces of waxed paper or plastic wrap. Pound until ⅓-inch thick. Place 1 slice of prosciutto and 1 slice of provolone on each chicken piece and roll up. Secure with toothpicks.

2. Combine flour, Parmesan cheese, salt and pepper in shallow bowl. (This can be made up to 2 to 3 days in advance.) Coat chicken in flour mixture. Reserve excess flour mixture.

3. Heat oil in large skillet over medium heat. Working in batches, brown chicken on both sides. Transfer to **CROCK-POT®** slow cooker. Add soup, wine, if desired, and sage. Cover; cook on LOW 5 to 7 hours or on HIGH 2 to 3 hours.

4. If desired, stir in 2 to 3 tablespoons reserved flour mixture. Cover; cook on LOW 15 minutes or until thickened.

Makes 6 servings

Sesame Chicken

4 chicken legs *or* 4 thighs and 4 drumsticks
4 bone-in chicken breasts
1 cup rice flour
8 teaspoons sesame seeds
  Salt and black pepper
  Vegetable oil
1 cup chicken broth
½ cup chopped celery
¼ cup chopped onion
1 teaspoon dried tarragon
¼ cup water
¼ cup cornstarch
1½ cups sour cream

1. Cut through joints to separate thighs and drumsticks. Combine rice flour, sesame seeds, salt and pepper in medium bowl. Dip chicken pieces in mixture to coat.

2. Heat oil in large skillet over medium heat. Working in batches, brown chicken on all sides. Transfer to paper towel-lined plate. Place in **CROCK-POT®** slow cooker.

3. Add broth, celery, onion and tarragon. Cover; cook on LOW 7 to 8 hours or on HIGH 3 to 4 hours.

4. Turn **CROCK-POT®** slow cooker to HIGH. Whisk water into cornstarch in small bowl until smooth. Add sour cream; mix well. Add to **CROCK-POT®** slow cooker; stir gently. Cover; cook 15 to 20 minutes or until thickened.

Makes 4 to 6 servings

Chipotle Chicken Casserole

1 pound boneless skinless chicken thighs, cubed
1 teaspoon salt
1 teaspoon ground cumin
1 bay leaf
1 canned chipotle pepper in adobo sauce, minced
1 onion, diced
1 can (about 15 ounces) navy beans, rinsed and drained
1 can (about 15 ounces) black beans, rinsed and drained
1 can (about 14 ounces) crushed tomatoes, undrained
1½ cups chicken broth
½ cup orange juice
¼ cup chopped fresh cilantro (optional)

Layer chicken, salt, cumin, bay leaf, chipotle pepper, onion, beans, tomatoes, broth and orange juice in **CROCK-POT®** slow cooker. Cover; cook on LOW 7 to 8 hours or on HIGH 3½ to 4 hours. Remove and discard bay leaf before serving. Garnish with cilantro, if desired.

Makes 6 servings

Spice It Up

Cheesy Corn and Peppers

2 pounds frozen corn

2 tablespoons butter, cut into cubes

2 poblano peppers, chopped *or* 1 green bell pepper and 1 jalapeño pepper, seeded and finely chopped*

1 teaspoon salt

½ teaspoon ground cumin

¼ teaspoon coarsely ground black pepper

1 cup (4 ounces) shredded sharp Cheddar cheese

3 ounces cream cheese, cut into cubes

Poblano and jalapeño peppers can sting and irritate the skin; wear rubber gloves when handling peppers and do not touch your eyes. Wash hands after handling.

1. Coat **CROCK-POT®** slow cooker with nonstick cooking spray. Combine all ingredients except Cheddar cheese and cream cheese in **CROCK-POT®** slow cooker. Cover; cook on HIGH 2 hours.

2. Stir in cheeses; cover and cook on HIGH 15 minutes or until melted.

Makes 8 servings

Hot Pot Noodle Soup

2 to 3 tablespoons peanut oil
2 onions, chopped
1 carrot, chopped
3 stalks lemongrass, thinly sliced
⅔ cup minced fresh ginger
8 cloves garlic, minced
7 whole star anise
3 quarts beef stock
3 tablespoons fish sauce (nam pla)*
1 package (12 ounces) fresh udon noodles or fresh linguine
1 tablespoon dark sesame oil
3 cups bean sprouts
4 green onions, sliced
4 serrano peppers, sliced**
6 tablespoons chopped fresh basil
6 tablespoons chopped fresh mint
6 tablespoons chopped fresh cilantro
Lime wedges

*Nam pla, Vietnamese fish sauce, can be found in the ethnic section of many grocery stores and in Asian markets.

**Serrano peppers can sting and irritate the skin, so wear rubber gloves when handling peppers and do not touch your eyes.

1. Heat peanut oil in large heavy saucepan over medium-high heat. Add onions, carrot, lemongrass, ginger, garlic and star anise; cook and stir until vegetables are softened. Transfer to **CROCK-POT®** slow cooker. Add stock and fish sauce. Cover; cook on LOW 7 to 9 hours or on HIGH 4 to 5 hours. Remove and discard star anise.

2. Cook noodles in large saucepan of boiling salted water until tender. Drain; rinse under cold water. Return to same saucepan. Toss noodles with sesame oil.

3. To serve, place noodles in bowls. Top with bean sprouts, green onions, serrano peppers, basil, mint and cilantro. Ladle soup over noodles and serve with lime wedges.

Makes 6 to 8 servings

Tip
Try this with pork, chicken or seafood, infusing the appropriate stock with the aromatic herbs and spices.

Polenta with Beef Chile Sauce

2 tablespoons vegetable oil

2 pounds boneless beef round roast, cut into bite-size pieces

1 yellow onion, finely chopped

2 cloves garlic, diced

1¾ cups water

5 canned whole mild green chiles, peeled and diced*

1 canned chipotle pepper in adobo sauce, diced*

1 teaspoon salt

1 teaspoon all-purpose flour

1 teaspoon dried oregano

½ teaspoon ground cumin

¼ teaspoon black pepper

1 package (16 ounces) prepared polenta

Fresh cilantro (optional)

*Green chiles and chipotle peppers can sting and irritate the skin, so wear rubber gloves when handling peppers and do not touch your eyes.

1. Heat oil in large skillet over medium heat. Working in batches, brown beef on all sides. Add onion and garlic during last few minutes of browning. Transfer to **CROCK-POT®** slow cooker.

2. Add water, chiles and chipotle pepper; mix well. Cover; cook on LOW 2 hours.

3. Combine salt, flour, oregano, cumin and black pepper in small bowl. Add to **CROCK-POT®** slow cooker; mix well. Cover; cook on LOW 3 to 4 hours.

4. Turn **CROCK-POT®** slow cooker to WARM. Preheat broiler. Slice polenta into ½-inch-thick rounds. Place on greased baking sheet. Broil until crispy, about 4 minutes on each side.

5. To serve, place polenta rounds on plates and spoon beef and sauce over top. Garnish with cilantro.

Makes 4 to 6 servings

Thai Shrimp Soup Infused with Lemongrass, Ginger and Chiles

¾ **pound large raw shrimp, peeled and deveined, shells reserved**

8 **cups fish stock or chicken stock**

1 **cup diced carrots**

3 **stalks lemongrass, thinly sliced**

2 to 3 **tablespoons grated fresh ginger**

2 **tablespoons minced garlic**

1 **can (about 14 ounces) unsweetened coconut milk**

1½ **tablespoons finely chopped fresh Thai basil** *or* **chopped fresh basil**

1½ **tablespoons finely chopped fresh mint**

1½ **tablespoons finely chopped fresh cilantro**

1 **serrano pepper, thinly sliced***

1 to 2 **limes, juiced**

¼ to ½ **teaspoon sambal oelek chile paste****

6 **thin lime slices**

Serrano peppers can sting and irritate the skin, so wear rubber gloves when handling peppers and do not touch your eyes.

**Chile pepper pastes, such as sambal oelek, are commonly used condiments in Southeast Asia. You can find them in the ethnic section of many grocery stores, in Asian markets or online.*

1. Halve shrimp lengthwise. Place in refrigerator.

2. Place shrimp shells, stock, carrots, lemongrass, ginger and garlic in **CROCK-POT®** slow cooker. Cover; cook on LOW 3½ to 4½ hours or on HIGH 2 to 3 hours.

3. Strain broth and return to **CROCK-POT®** slow cooker; discard solids. Add coconut milk, shrimp, basil, mint, cilantro, serrano pepper, lime juice and chile paste. Cover; cook on HIGH 15 minutes or until shrimp are pink and opaque.

4. Ladle soup into bowls and garnish with lime slices.

Makes 6 servings

Mexican Cornbread Pudding

1 can (about 14 ounces) cream-style corn

2 eggs

1 can (4 ounces) diced mild green chiles, drained

¾ cup yellow cornmeal

2 tablespoons sugar

2 tablespoons vegetable oil

2 teaspoons baking powder

¾ teaspoon salt

½ cup (2 ounces) shredded Cheddar cheese

Coat 2-quart **CROCK-POT®** slow cooker with nonstick cooking spray. Combine corn, eggs, chiles, cornmeal, sugar, oil, baking powder and salt in medium bowl. Pour into **CROCK-POT®** slow cooker. Cover; cook on LOW 2 to 2½ hours or until center is set. Sprinkle cheese over top. Cover and let stand 5 minutes or until cheese is melted.

Makes 8 servings

Black Bean Soup

3 cans (about 15 ounces each) black beans, rinsed and draind

3½ cups beef stock

½ pound bacon, crisp-cooked and crumbled

1 onion, chopped

4 plum tomatoes, diced

⅓ cup red wine vinegar

2 jalapeño peppers, minced*

1½ teaspoons ground cumin

1 teaspoon dried oregano

1 teaspoon dried thyme

Kosher salt and black pepper

Diced avocado, lime juice and shredded Cheddar cheese

Jalapeño peppers can sting and irritate the skin, so wear rubber gloves when handing peppers and do not touch eyes.

1. Combine beans, stock, bacon, onion, tomatoes, vinegar, jalapeño peppers, cumin, oregano and thyme in **CROCK-POT®** slow cooker. Cover; cook on LOW 8 to 10 hours or on HIGH 4 to 5 hours.

2. Season with salt and black pepper. Serve with avocado, lime juice and cheese.

Makes 4 to 6 servings

Index